Abba
Father

Reflections and
Prayers from
a Simpler Time

William DeWitt Hyde
Edited by Hal M. Helms

PARACLETE PRESS
BREWSTER, MASSACHUSETTS

Library of Congress Cataloging-in-Publication Data

Hyde, William De Witt, 1858-1917.
Abba Father: Reflections and prayers from a simpler time/
William De Witt Hyde: edited by Hal M. Helms.
        p. cm.
        ISBN 1-55725-200-9   (pbk.)
        1. Christian life. 2. Devotional exercises. I. Helms, Hal
McElwaine. II. Title.
BV4501.H89 1998
242'.8–dc21
                                                    98-4937
                                                    CIP

Graphics on pages 5, 7, 9, 13, 17, 25, 31, 43, 61, 65, 71: Corel Corporation.

10 9 8 7 6 5 4 3

© 1998 by Paraclete Press
ISBN: 1-55725-200-9

Published by Paraclete Press
Brewster, Massachusetts
www.paraclete-press.com

Printed in the United States of America

Table of Contents

Preface

To walk and talk with God, as child with father, friend with friend; lifting up life into the light of his love—this is religion. Instead of criticism of it, commentary upon it, controversy over it, philosophy about it, exhortation to it, of which the world is full, this little book offers religion itself, just as one would offer a picture, a story, or a song.

Real religion is the offering up of each man's life, in its concrete setting, day by day, hour by hour, moment by moment, to the guidance and keeping of God. Thus each man's religion, like his life, is individual, unique.

As such, however, it is incommunicable. Consequently, when one would share it with others, as in public worship, many experiences and needs of many men must be thrown together into a composite expression. This of course is the way liturgies and books of common prayer are formed.

Admirably adapted as they are for uniting at one time and place the many aspirations of many hearts, they too have their limitations. Amid such a kaleidoscopic variety and succession of petition and praise, the mind, unless it be unusually nimble and alert, becomes distracted. As Mr. Arthur C. Benson has said, "To follow a service with uplifted attention requires more mental agility than I possess; point after point is raised, and yet, if one pauses to meditate, to wonder, to aspire, one is lost, and misses the thread of the service." Still, for public worship the liturgy, with all these obvious defects, is the best thing we have—even though it must ever be a service more of the emotions than of the mind.

Midway between the concrete religion of active life and the abstract, composite liturgy, there is a form of worship adapted to the individual in the quiet hour. It takes a single aspect of our common experience at a time, holds it before the mind in logical development and sustained attention, and thus with mind and heart together lifts it into the light of the divine. As a result, one finds that when in concrete life a case arises which belongs to the class of experiences which has been made the subject of such communion with the Father, one's attitude towards that case is changed. In other words prayer of this sort is answered, if less obviously and directly, no less satisfactorily and surely, than prayer which offers the concrete situation of the immediate moment directly to the divine control.

These essay meditations, or sermon prayers, are the outcome of a year of enforced rest—cut off from ordinary work on the one hand, and attendance upon public worship on the other. They were conceived in the gardens and chapels of Oxford and written in Switzerland, at Burghalde, the site of a medieval castle near Oberhofen on Lake Thun. If they shall reveal to anyone the simplicity and comprehensiveness, the modesty and grandeur, the peace and power, of the Christian life, my period of exile will not have been unfruitful; I shall have proved a brother workman of the Swiss peasants with whom I exchanged greetings as we met on the way to our different tasks, and Eiger, Monk and Jungfrau will not have reflected to my castle-site the Alpine glow in vain.

William DeWitt Hyde
Bowdoin College
Brunswick, Maine
August, 1908

An Invitation

In these brief meditations, you are invited to allow your mind and heart to unite in thinking quietly about the many facets which make up your life. Surely our life in this world is "a many-splendored thing." Holding life up to the light of God, thinking about what it means to be a human person and a child of God, we are strengthened in our best resolves and helped in our desire to leave behind the sordid or selfish patterns we may have developed along the way.

Meditation is not an easy indulgence in reverie. It is not nostalgia, looking at life through rose-tinted glasses. It is an engagement with the depths within, an attempt to unite our hearts to our heads, our thinking and our feeling, so that we become more whole, more integrated, more what we were created to be.

This little volume can help begin or continue that process. It may be useful to take one subject at a time, letting the thoughts recorded here inspire your thoughts beyond the written page, to engage with your divine Creator in the splendid work he has permitted you to do: to come to know him and yourself in reality and in truth.

Hal M. Helms
June, 1997

Gratitude

Almighty and Loving Creator

I thank you for this glorious world in which I live—
for the mountain and valley,
rock and soil,
forest and field,
river and sea,
sun and rain,
flower and fruit,
plant and animal.

I thank you for the great social institutions built like walls
along life's highway to keep my feet from straying into sin—
home and school,
church and state,
law and custom,
art and literature,
history and science.

I thank you for the education that comes
through parents and teachers;
through success and failure;
through legal compulsion and social expectation;
through rewarded right and punished wrong.

I thank you for the men and women walking by my side along
the dusty road of life

who do your will so patiently and modestly,
so sweetly that I cannot fail to feel its charm.
Most of all I thank you for Jesus Christ—
that he once for all revealed the eternal supremacy
of love, truth and purity
over hardness and brutality,
pride and hypocrisy,
tyranny and superstition.
I thank you that he won for the world this spiritual victory
when it meant the crown of thorns,
the scourging,
the spear point,
and the cross.

May I show my gratitude by the good use I make
of all natural resources—
by my appreciation of the beautiful in nature and in art;
by my obedience to all just laws and beneficent institutions;
by struggling for the world's improvement;
by helping its tried and tempted souls;
and doing all in my power
to lead men and women in the direction marked out
by the precept and example,
the service and sacrifice of Christ.

Thus may I show your goodness to other's souls;
that they may come to the glad and grateful
sense of being
sons and daughters,
brothers and sisters
in the divine-human family.

Sin

Most Merciful Father

Poor and unworthy has been my use of your good gifts.
Your will is perfect love to all your children.
All that falls short of such love is sin.
Yet I fall short all the time.

In hours of dullness I cannot even so much as see your will,
much less feel the promptings of your love.
In moments when passion sweeps through me uncontrolled,
I spread bitterness and sorrow far and wide
in the hearts of your other children.

In season of weakness I am unequal to doing the duty
that I see.
In fits of excitement I do not stop to think
of the cruel misery my hasty words and deeds inflict.
In periods of depression I give up all attempt
to be more than the selfish animal
my brutish inheritances make it so natural for me to be.

The opportunities for kindness slip away unimproved,
and sad hearts are left uncomforted,
wrongs are left unrebuked,
duties are left undone;
the world is poorer,
your children the more wretched for what I fail to do.

Worse than all are the meanness,
the selfishness,
the greed,
the lust,
the malice,
the jealousy,
the pride,
that lead me to gain for myself some petty pleasure
by another's pain;
some trifling profit by another's loss,
some gratification of passion, at the price
of another's degradation;
some miserable gain for myself and my family
bought by corrupting the government;
some ignoble sense of personal elevation won
by pulling other people down.

For these outcroppings of inherited animalism;
for slothfulness and shirking;
for wanton self-indulgence in reckless sacrifice
of others' rights;
for responsibility for the world's sufferings and wrongs;

forgive me, even as I in turn forgive those who do me injury.

Thorns

Father of Justice and Kindness

To each child of yours,
as the price of sensitiveness that feels your leading,
or the effectiveness that does your will,
you give some thorn to prick the surface of pride.

Whether it be quick temper,
intense passions,
extreme shyness,
physical defect,
mental dullness,
lack of early advantages,
uncongenial relatives,
unhappy marriage,
a wayward child,
loss of fortune,
inability to get work,
alienation of friends through hopeless misunderstanding,
or bereavement tearing up the very roots of the soul—

to each you send his thorn,
either secretly buried in the sensitive flesh,
or woven into the crown to be worn openly upon the brow.

Help me to extract from mine its lesson of humility.

If it unfits me for the large sphere I should choose,
surely you have some modest place for me to fill,
some humble task for me to do,
with which my defects,
my misfortunes,
my blunders,
even my repented sins cannot interfere.
Help me to take it cheerfully, leaving to others
the larger service I forego.

Grant that my own secret sorrow,
my own keen disappointment,
may make me sympathetic to discover,
tactful to treat,
the suffering that lies,
hidden or exposed, in every human heart.

Thus, even through sorrow—merited or unmerited—
I may be drawn closer to you,
closer to the suffering Christ,
closer to my needy fellowmen.

Through a deeper tenderness,
a profounder humility,
a broader charity,
a gentler helpfulness,
may I find in the heightened joy of the devoted spirit
abundant compensation for the suffering
of the outward man.

Patience

Eternal God

Thousands of centuries you have waited for the little good
thus far achieved upon this earth.

For you love the partial good painfully wrought out
in freedom
more than the greatest mechanical perfection.

You have trusted the welfare of your children
to their own weak, erring hands.

For ages, in brutal sensuality and barbaric cruelty,
they have worked havoc upon each other,
and brought shame upon themselves.

Even now millions of your children are plunged
in hopeless degradation.

All around us, even in the most civilized races
and the most cultivated lands,
the lives of those we know and love
are embittered by unconquered animalism in themselves,
or surviving brutality in others.

When I join with others of like mind in efforts
to do a little good,
our labors are thwarted
by our own weakness,
by the powers of evil,
or by the indifference of those worst enemies of progress—
the people who think themselves and the world
good enough already.

In the face of difficulty,
discouragement,
misunderstanding,
misrepresentation,
help me to go on doing my best
in patient perseverance;
even though the only visible outcome
is the continued victory of evil.

Give me the assurance that every good as well as every
evil influence counts;
and that the result shall represent all the forces put forth
on both sides,
of which my effort for the right
is one.

Thus may I play an apparently losing game as steadily
and bravely
as one where I appear to win,
knowing that you are on the side of the good;
that good has a uniting,
lasting,
spreading,
reproducing,
conquering
POWER
evil can never have.

Toiling in your patience and your perseverance,
may I share, even in the struggle,
your triumph
and your peace.

Enemies

Father of All

We are all dear to you.
Yet we are selfish,
shortsighted,
petty,
continually tempted to be mean.

Partly through my fault,
partly through the fault of others,
I clash with them, and they with me;
and they become my enemies.

In so far as their enmity is due to any fault of mine,
may I promptly humble myself,
ask their forgiveness,
and do my best to make amends.

May I count no humiliation or sacrifice too great
a price to pay
for the restoration of goodwill whenever by any act of mine,
whether of omission or commission,
it has been forfeited.

May I remember that I cannot be right with you,
so long as I am wrong towards any of your children.

When others are at fault,
when they hate me without cause,
when they persist in wronging me,
when they misrepresent as evil the good I try to do—
while I defend my rights with firmness,
may I be free from personal bitterness.

May I never forget that my enemy is more than
his wrong attitude towards me;
may I remember that he is your child, my brother,
that he still has some good qualities,
and is capable of more.

Thus even when compelled to oppose him,
may I in courtesy and kindness
show myself a friend to his better self,
and win or at least deserve
the restoration of his esteem.

While friendly even to my enemies,
and peaceable with all men,
when duty requires
may I not shrink from making enemies.

When the cruel oppress the innocent,
when the dishonest cheat the poor,
when the strong trample the weak,
when the incompetent hold office,
when the licentious break down the family,
when the corrupt undermine the state—
then may I be bold to rebuke,
to prosecute,
to punish,
welcoming their enmity as the price
every brave man must pay,
as Christ paid it,
for living your life
and doing your will
in a world of selfishness and sin.

Forgiveness

Most Merciful Father

You forgive me so far as I am truly penitent.

May I likewise forgive all who sin against me,
all who sin against society,
all who sin against you,
even as you forgive me and them.

Help me to remember that the great evils
are not wrought in deliberate malice,
but in unimaginative selfishness,
in wrath,
greed,
and lust.

Finding the survivals of savagery and animality
within myself,
may I have charity for the outbreaks of these
hereditary traits in others,
who perchance have had less help than I from home,
school,
society,
moral influence,
and spiritual inspiration.

May I count no sin too heinous to pardon,
no man too hardened to reclaim,
no person too fallen to uplift.

When I forgive the penitent,
help me to stand against a hard and unforgiving world.
Help me in sacrificial sympathy to bear with him
the penalties formal justice may deem necessary to inflict,
and to share with him
the condemnation a merciless public is ever ready to impose.

Thus may I make my forgiveness a reality in the actual world,
and open the door of genuine social restoration
to those who have gone astray.

Yet may I not lose sight of moral distinctions
in a mush of sentimentality.

When public protection requires the punishment of a criminal,
the correction of the depraved,
the discharge of the inefficient,
the prosecution of the dishonest,
the exposure of the corrupt—
may I be stern and hard towards them,
even while I have in my heart the tenderest charity
for those I cause to suffer,
and whose suffering
I sympathetically share.

Forgiveness

Thus may I in my little world,
as you in your great universe,
blend severest justice with gentlest mercy,
inexorable penalty with absolute forgiveness,
inflicting pain unflinchingly
when love prescribes it for society's protection
and the offender's good.

Work

Creator and Ruler of All

I thank you for the sunshine
with its stored-up heat in wood and coal;
for the power in falling water,
expanding steam,
and electricity;
for timber and minerals;
for cotton, silk, and linen;
for meat and grain,
for fruit and vegetable.

Still more I thank you that the final touch
which transforms these materials into use,
and gives to each his share in the produce
of the whole world's work
at the time and place where it is wanted—
that agriculture,
manufacture,
transportation,
and exchange,
are left to be furnished by the hand and brain of man.

Help me to find my chief delight in work
wherein I join my hand,
my brain,
my heart,

to your power,
your laws,
your love.

May I choose that task which most taxes
my highest powers,
and best serves the world's deepest need.

May I do it with such skill,
such thoroughness,
such joy,
that it shall have about it
the strength of the mountains,
the freedom of the streams,
the gladness of the sunshine,
the fertility of the fields,
the beauty of the stars and flowers.

Thus may I become not a mere creature but a creator,
not one of your works,
but one of your coworkers.
Help me to do good, full-measured work,
when poor, scant work brings equal pay.

May I give a full equivalent for all I take,
add to the world's wealth as much as I consume,
and be a sound member of the economic order.

Work

May I be fair to my employer,
whether he treats me well or ill;
considerate to my employees,
whether they love or hate me;
loyal to my fellow-workmen,
whether they stand by me or not.

May I be just to those distant consumers of my product
who will never know to whose honesty and honor
they owe the sound quality of the goods I make
and the service I render them.

Play

Lord of the Sunrise and Sunset

Though it is honest work that gives me my place
in your great universe,
yet what I can do is so little,
what I can do well is so monotonous,
that when I devote myself to work alone
I become a mere pin-point in your mighty mechanism:

I lose firmness of nerves,
resourcefulness of mind,
decisiveness of will,
range of imagination,
quickness of sympathy;
I offer to my friends,
I hand down to my children,
a shriveled heart and a deadened mind.

Therefore I thank you for the great privilege of play:
for the sports that take me to the field,
the forest,
the river,
and the sea;
for the games that call out courage, endurance, and skill,
in friendly contests, physical and mental.

I thank you for the ordered play of mind and soul in art:
for architecture,
sculpture,
and painting;
for music and poetry;
for the novel and drama—
for the power they have to set before us beauty and harmony,
to interpret love and heroism,
to take us into the intense, typical experiences of humanity,
and send us back to our individual lives,
enlarged,
enriched,
with a clearer vision of the noble,
a truer scorn of what is base.

At the same time, save me from making play the end of life,
to the distaste of work
and the neglect of duty.
Save me from the base desire to gain in play
what others lose.

Save me from all pleasure that involves loss, pain,
or degradation to another.

May work and play in healthy alternation
become expressions of my joy
in using the powers you have given me,
and my delight
in the world which you have made.

Play

Help me to keep on gaining new interests through life,
and carry the child's heart into old age.

Grant me the strong constitution,
the cheerful disposition,
the steady will,
the sympathetic heart,
which are play's appropriate gifts—
that I may be what you would have me be,
as well as do what you would have me do.

Health

Loving Father

You have made health the normal condition of every child of obedient parents, who themselves obey your laws of diet, exercise, rest, recreation, cheerfulness, trust and love.

Teach me to obey these laws,
and when I disobey,
to profit by the swift, sure penalty which mercifully follows.

Save me from the folly of treating bodily symptoms which spring from spiritual sins
by drugs, opiates, narcotics, and intoxicants,
in a futile endeavor to call in matter and mechanism
to make good defects of mind and heart.

May I cure gluttony by temperance,
idleness by exercise,
overwork by rest,
anger by gentleness,
worry by trust,
depression by hope,
fear by faith,
hate by love.

Yet when accident, exposure, or overstrain has broken
or deranged the normal structure of my body;
when contagion has introduced hostile organisms
and noxious substances into my blood;
then may I treat broken bones and depleted tissues
as I would a broken bridge or a washed-out road-bed,
by appropriate material means;
then may I fight bacteria with physical weapons
as I would wolves and lions.

In this fight may I use with gratitude
all the aids of medical skill and science you have
placed within reach,
honoring the men and women whose study and practice
of this beneficent art
make victory possible.

Thus with mind and heart rightly related to you,
to your laws,
and to the people with whom I live and work,
with the aid in emergencies of scientific medicine,
may I be doubly fortified against disease;
may I be blessed with that abounding health
which is the secret of individual happiness
and social usefulness.

$\mathcal{T}$ravel

Father of the Whole Human Family

When I remain too long at home my own importance swells to
unseemly proportions,
and the vision of your greatness fades.
Then may I leave the spot where I have come to fancy myself
the center of a little world,
and humbly accept some place on the circumference
of your great universe.

Then may I behold your glory on the mountain and the sea,
feel your quiet by the forest or the lake,
trace your justice as other men and nations have expressed it in
customs and institutions different from my own,
gaze on beauty as you have wrought it
into the forms of nature
and the features of men and women,
or as genius has reflected it in art.

Yet forbid that I degenerate into the chronic traveler,
living only to be sumptuously fed,
softly bedded,
periodically transported,
perpetually amused.

May I strictly subordinate the brief days of travel
to long weeks of life and work at home,
ever going for the sake of the healthier,

stronger,
wiser,
happier return.

While viewing the works of other men and women
may I ever be planning improvement of my own,
justifying temporary absence from my specific duties
by the increased vigor and enthusiasm
with which they are resumed.

Even when the old ties of home and family are broken,
when the scale of living must be reduced to match
decreasing income,
may I refuse to be a runaway,
but count the humblest usefulness at home more honorable
than the most luxurious idleness of exile.

Going and coming, at home and abroad,
may I everywhere be
your grateful and obedient child,
remembering
that contemplation of your works must prove its worth
by the constancy with which I fill the place
where you have put me,
and the fidelity with which I do the specific work
you have given me to do.

Faith

Eternal Wisdom

Give me the faith that dares to doubt all that refuses
to takes its place in a coherent whole of history and science,
all that declines to justify its claims in reason's open court.
For reason in me and in others is the reflection
of that complete reason
which is your mind.

Yet while nothing that contradicts true reason and wisdom can
be true,
your experience infinitely transcends ours,
and what seems evil from our partial point of view
may serve a good purpose in your larger plan.

May I seek to see your hand
in circumstances and conditions which seem
to defy my human reason,
and begin to trust that there is a sacredness in life
and infinite grace at work in your world.

May I begin to doubt the subtle lie
that wrong shall ultimately prevail,
because there is so much suffering and cruelty in your world.

May I have eyes to see that you have not abandoned
your creation,
and that we still move toward the time
when your glory will cover the earth as waters cover the seas.

This is not an easy faith, Father,
and sometimes I grow disillusioned
and even join those who accuse you of having left us
to our tormentors.

But I choose to look up, beyond the sordidness of the world,
and I choose to believe that your purpose will prevail.

In the meantime, strengthen my faith and lead me onward
to the goal you have for me.

$\mathcal{H}$ope

God of Hope

The vision of faith fades;
the triumph of the good is long deferred;
reform is defeated;
progress is slow;
disaster falls;
degeneration sets in.
Criticism shows that even our saints and heroes were men
of like passions with ourselves,
idealized by time, distance and human admiration.

Passing from the warm atmosphere of faith into the hard, cold
world of fact,
a chill strikes to the heart of all my cherished convictions,
and they vanish into empty dreams.
Business,
politics,
society,
education,
even religion,
seem to be in the hands of men who see nothing higher than
profit and popularity, or at best, tradition and convention.
The opportunist defeats the statesman;
the fraudulent contractor and dishonest promoter
drive the honest dealer and the upright businessman
to the wall;

polite pretentiousness takes precedence over genuine worth
in marriage and social position;
the self-seeking priest sits in the seat of the prophet.

When such observations weigh me down, give me the hope
that sees through present evil the sure triumph of the
coming good. Show me that these evils always have been;
and in spite of them, better conditions, larger liberties, happier
homes, higher characters, nobler institutions,
have steadily emerged.

Give me the assurance that, in ways I cannot comprehend,
your love will work good out of evil. Help me to live in
constant foretaste of the better order my faith and hope
and love shall help to usher in.
Yet save me from the folly that would keep out evil
by shutting its own silly eyes.
May I hope for a good, not apart from evil,
not won without struggle,
not miraculously projected into this world,
or supernaturally set up in the next—
but for a good wrought out in struggle against evil
by willing hands,
sturdy wills,
and loving hearts.

$\mathcal{L}$ove

Loving God

I thank you for the bond of marriage which seals
the mutual affection of man and woman into lifelong devotion,
and perpetuates it in offspring.
May I think and speak of this relationship wherein we share
your creative power,
ever with reverence and honor,
never with levity or shame.

You have entrusted this holy office of creative love
to the coarse hands of men and women,
and wantonly have they perverted it.
You only know the beastliness and cruelty,
the bitterness and agony,
the sin and shame,
the despair and degradation
the perversion of this function has entailed.

May I see the love between husband and wife as
the crowning evidence of your creative love,
and cherish the lifelong union in mutual affection
of one man and one woman
as one of life's supreme blessings.

May this love be so deep and sweet and pure
that it shall overflow into intimate friendship with other men
and women,
into fondness for little children,
banishing all jealously and selfishness
and ushering in the reign of universal love.

Family

Father of All

I thank you for the common life of the family flowing freely
through each member's heart,
bringing diversity of age,
gender,
experience,
strength,
wisdom,
beauty,
innocence,
vivacity,
charm,
as an offering to each
and the property of all.

Help me gladly to give up all merely private interests so far as
they conflict with the common life, counting the least I
can do for my family more precious than the greatest
pleasure to be found apart from them.

May I leave other members free to make their contribution
to the daily life in their own way, using constraint only with
the very young, who have not learned the sweet law of love
which binds the conduct of each to the service of all.

May I cheerfully endure the drudgery and privation,
the clash of taste and temperament, which the molding
of many into one in this intimate relationship involves.
Teach me at the same time love's larger lesson,
that as the individual gains his true life in the family
by giving up his selfish life,
so the family gains by every pure friendship,
every noble artistic interest,
every generous social service in which parent or child,
husband or wife, shares and serves the larger life outside.

Even if circumstances do not permit me to enter
this holiest bond,
may I revere it and cherish it for others.

Having once entered it, may I never relapse into
the old selfish attitude,
never again estimate profit and loss in the old
individualistic terms.

May I give all, finding in opportunity for larger
giving my chief return.

Only when cruelty,
lust,
drunkenness,
or settled hate make love impossible,
beyond the power of patience and charity to restore,
may I, whether for myself or for another,
turn to divorce for such relief from intolerable degradation as
the law,
in the interest of the decency and dignity of true marriage,
mercifully grants.

Duty

Lord and Lifegiver

I thank you for the place where you have put me,
with persons on every side whom I must either serve
or injure,
work which I must do whether well or ill,
things I must either beautify or mar.

It is at once your will and my duty to treat these persons
so kindly,
to do this work so well,
to order these things so nicely,
that happiness, goodness, beauty
shall be the harmonious result.

Help me to contribute with joy my little part to
your vast harmony.

When my little plans clash with your larger purposes,
may I gladly give up my personal preference to serve
your mighty aims,
and find therein not hardship, but delight.

Yet save me from the fanaticism that would take on duties
beyond my strength.
Modestly contrasting my limitations with your infinity,
may I confine myself to the tasks you clearly lay upon me,
and at the same time give me strength to do.

As duty faithfully and lovingly performed is my own highest good,
may I count it the best thing I can provide
for my family,
my children,
my friends.

May I not in false self-sacrifice do so much for them,
and so shield them,
as to deprive them of their highest privilege
and best education:
the doing of their own hard duties in the loving spirit
which takes away their hardness and transforms them into joy.

When duties clash,
when I can do but one of the things I feel I ought to do,
then may I be fair both to others and to myself.
May I ask which duty, in the same circumstances,
I would advise my best friend to do;
may I do that duty decisively,
without regrets for what is left undone,
knowing that what I would advise another whom I love is,
so far as I can ascertain it,
what *your* love would have me choose and do.

Sacrifice

Father and Giver of Life

Your perfection is not the perfection of a finished thing,
but the perfection of a living person—
the perfection of a love that seeks through struggle,
opposition,
suffering,
the best that human freedom working with natural resources
can achieve.

In calling me to share this perfect purpose,
you often require me to live up to what would be good
for me as an individual,
that I may do more for the good of others
and the welfare of your world.

Help me so to see the beauty of your life,
so to feel the drawing of your love,
that I may gladly make the sacrifices love requires—
ever remembering that my brothers and sisters are as dear to
you as I,
and that I am your child only so far as I share your love for
them.

When they are in poverty or sickness,
when they are downtrodden or maltreated,
when my family needs me,
when my country calls,

when great public issues are at stake,
when truth needs an interpreter
or right a defender—
then may I freely give time,
strength,
money,
influence,
if need be health
and life itself,
to the larger work,
finding in the greater gain to my brothers,
in the benefit of society,
and in fellowship with you
such ample compensation as shall make the yoke of service
easy,
and the burden of sacrifice light.

At the same time save me from making sacrifice
an end in itself,
or seeking it as a means of securing your favor.
I am as dear to you as are those I serve;
you delight not in sacrifice as such,
but only in the love it springs from
and the good it does.

Sacrifice

Since I am responsible for my own health,
happiness,
efficiency,
and development
as no one else can be,
may every sacrifice I make be justified by some greater good
done to others
in fulfillment of your equal love to them and me.

Courage

Father, Refuge of Those Who Seek You

Give me the courage never to be content with things
as they are,
or myself as I am,
but ever to welcome your call to progress and reform.

I like to do things I can do easily because I have done them
before;
you are ever calling me to do new things,
for which I have no ready-made aptitude.

I like to do things which everybody will approve, because they
are familiar;
you are ever calling me to do new things
which the good misunderstand
and the evil misinterpret.

I like to do things that succeed,
because the world wants them;
you are ever calling me to do new things
for which the world is not quite ready,
and therefore at the outset are doomed to fail.

Give me the brave heart to rise above the cowardice men
call conservatism,
and obey your call.
Teach me that only by attempting what seems impossible
can power be gained or great good accomplished,
that only by disregarding at times the praise
and blame of men
can your voice be heard aright,
that only by risking occasional defeat in minor battles
can the great campaign be won.

Still save me from arrogance,
foolhardiness
and fanaticism.
You are a General considerate of your soldiers.
Make me content with the work of one man,
for which you have given me strength;
not falsely ambitious to do the work of ten.

Give me your patience with such wrongs as I am powerless to
remove.
Help me to keep in training and condition,
cheerful in the monotony of daily drill,
yielding neither to my own restlessness nor the rash
importunity of others,
waiting under arms for your command.

Courage

When your clear orders come,
doubly attested by manifest duty without
and the stirring of latent power within,
then may I have the courage which implicitly obeys,
counts no cost,
and fears no foe,
and leaves results entirely in your hands.

Humility

Eternal God, Friend of the Lowly

May I ever measure myself by the distance I fall short
of that perfect love
which is at once what you are,
and what I ought to be.
When measured by this true standard I am wholly wanting;
yet may I not be cast down.

For when I confess my weakness, then through
your grace am I strong.
For you are ever patient with me,
as a father with the unfulfilled promise of his child.
I am dear to you,
not mainly for the little that I do aright,
but for my penitence after doing wrong,
for my desire to do better,
for what in due time with your help I shall become.

Help me to keep this humility I learn from you
in my attitude towards my fellow men.
May I never try to pass with them as better than
you see me to be.
May I esteem them better than myself,
having reverence and tenderness for all,
pride and uncharitableness towards none.

With friends whom I can trust may I be frank about my shortcomings as I am with you.
Especially in the home,
and those intimate friendships where concealment is impossible,
may I welcome the light love sheds on my faults—
welcome even the pain love inflicts in healing surgery.

When enemies and censorious critics detect me
in some fault,
and try to break me down,
then may the humility I have learned from you become
my armor and defense.
Knowing how light are their worst charges
in comparison to what you know against me,
and in spite of knowing still forgive,
still love,
may I be strong in the confidence that no weakness
acknowledged,
no fault confessed,
no mistake corrected,
no sin repented,
can ever separate me from you
or from the friends you give to all who walk in true humility.

Injustice

Father of Truth and Mercy

Help me to face the fact of obvious injustice
in the tangled external world.
Crime for the most part goes unpunished,
wrong unredressed. Our lame and tardy justice overtakes
only the simpler sort of rascals who happen also to be fools.

The dishonest director,
the fraudulent promoter,
who spread poverty over thousands of homes,
live in luxurious wealth, envied and admired.
The seducer,
the patronizer of prostitution,
wrecks a whole life, or degrades a whole class of women,
yet passes as respectable.
The scandal-monger ruins reputations,
yet is tolerated in good society.

So interrelated are the forces of the world,
so interwoven are the lives of men,
so vast are the evils that flow from small sources,
so free are best and worst alike to meddle with the delicate
mechanism of society,
that on every side the innocent suffer for the greed and lust,
the meanness and fraud,
of guilty men who escape outward punishment.

On the other hand
virtue for the most part goes without its immediate outward
reward.
Patient toil is doomed to lifelong poverty.
Purity suffers the penalty of others' lust.
The genius, giving his best to art or science,
dies unrecognized.
The reformer fights a losing battle against entrenched
tradition and corruption.
Save me from the base belief that because things are so bad it is
useless to try to make them better.
Save me from the unbelief,
openly avowed or veiled in pious phrases,
which seeks material answers to spiritual questions,
physical rewards for moral qualities.

Knowing not how I could make a better world,
even with omnipotence to help,
believing that freedom with all its injustices is better than
the most perfect mechanism,
help me to accept injustice as the price of freedom
in a complex society,
which neither for myself,
nor for those I love, can I altogether escape.

Justice

Father of Truth and Justice

Finding in the outer world so much injustice,
I turn to the inner justice which consists in the soul's
relation to you.

In conscious fellowship with you
may I find the sure and sufficient reward of all virtue.
In exclusion from your life of love,
in blindness of eye and hardness of heart,
may I see the fearful and unescapable penalty
of persistent sin.

Show me that the dishonest man can have no real part or lot in
that beneficent economic order which you are building up on
earth,
and he is breaking down.

Show me that the corrupt politician can have no part or lot in
the patriot's love of country,
which he is helping to destroy.

Show me that the libertine's sodden soul can have
no part or lot
in the sweet joys of pure affection within the happy home,
which his conduct wrecks.

Show me that pride and greed,
deceit and hate,
can have no part or lot in that devotion to others
wherein the fellowship of your love is found.
On the other hand,
in all apparently unrewarded labor for truth,
beauty,
purity,
and love;
in all losing battles for the right;
in all defeated efforts for reform;
in all unsuccessful endeavors for the better order
that is yet to be;
sustain and comfort me with the sense that you are with me,
that even through sacrifice,
disaster,
defeat,
and death,
I am partaker in your triumph,
agent of your progress,
sharer of your life,
child of your love.
In the vision of your beauty granted to the pure in heart,
in the sharing of your love offered to the doers of your will,
may I find, as opposite sides of the same relationship,
your justice
and my own blessedness.

I thank you, too, that, tardily and indirectly,
even material goods and social honors
sometimes follow in the train of the inner justice
which binds the faithful soldier-soul to you.

Temperance

Father, Giver of Life that is Life Indeed

Help me to make my rule of life
the great law you have wrought into the structure of crystal,
plant and animal—the law man must embody in everything he
would make fit for use
and crown with beauty,
the law that grants to each detail
just so much as best serves the inner purpose
that animates the whole.

In diet may I eat and drink, in quality and quantity,
so much as will give the finest vigor of body and of mind—
not falling short through excessive restraint,
nor running to excess in gluttony and drunkenness.

In dress may I seek such texture, color and form as befits
my work and station, conforms to the customs of my fellows,
and makes attractive my personal appearance—
not falling short in slovenliness and eccentricity,
nor overdressing in vanity and ostentation.

In action may I exert my powers up to the limit of health
and the demands of my calling,
not shirking through laziness
nor wearing myself out with inordinate ambition.

In business may I seek so much money as will best serve
my family,
my community,
my social circle—
not content with less than is essential to efficiency,
nor anxious for more than I can organize into wholesome use
and rational enjoyment.

In society may I share my life with as many as I can touch with
sympathy and stimulus,
not drawing into my shell in selfish isolation,
nor squandering my independence in the chase for popularity.

In education may I learn for myself
and teach to my children
all that develops power and pleasure,
not neglecting any genuine intellectual interest,
nor sacrificing vitality and joy for rank and reputation.

In religion may I bring my conscious conduct
and my unconscious motivation
under the influence of your perfect love—
not lapsing into soulless secularity,
nor yet losing in mystic ecstasy the crowning grace
of practicality.

Responsibility

Father of All Mankind

Amid the many clashing forces
which together constitute the world,
some of which make for life, health, peace, joy,
others for discord, disease, misery, death—
grant that the little I can do may be
sweet,
sound,
just,
generous,
allied to the great stream of force making for good
which is your will.

This once secured,
may I drop at your feet my burden of responsibility,
knowing that in any event the issue is never the result
of my single effort
but the result of ten thousand forces
of which my act is only one.

When the event is outwardly and visibly successful,
may I not be puffed up
but rather modestly thankful for the other conditions which
make the success of my effort possible,
humbly grateful for the privilege of sharing
in an achievement
which is mainly yours.

When the event is an apparent failure,
may I have the assurance that it is due to factors which I did
not contribute, and could not control,
that in spite of this particular defeat
the powers of good are so much stronger,
the powers of evil so much weaker,
for the good effort I put forth.

May I work at the never-completed task of bringing
the better out of the worse,
assured that he who struggles to make the world materially
and morally better thereby dwells in fellowship with you
who are the spiritual best.

Though new forms of evil arise as fast as the old
are overthrown;
though as long as man is free and society grows more
and more complex,
evil will spread and the triumph of the good will be deferred;
may I never despair,
never deem the work too great for me to undertake,
or my power too small to count.
May I assume no entire responsibility whatever
for more than that,
casting all responsibility for the total outcome where it
belongs—
on you.

Wealth

Father

I thank you for your great economic law,
the law which thieves in various disguises may tamper with,
but never can destroy—
the law that in return for the goods or services I render
to the world,
the world stands ready to give me an equivalent,
whenever in the symbolic form of money I present my claim.

I thank you too for the saved wealth of ancestors
which came to me unearned.
Yet this more perilous gift I receive with fear and trembling.
For as this inheritance represents the surplus of their service to
the world
above personal consumption,
so it brings to me the temptation to make my consumption
exceed my production,
and thus become a bankrupt and a beggar
in my account with the world of services rendered
and received.
Forbid that I become a spiritual pauper through misuse
of wealth
by gaining which, my ancestors proved themselves
the world's benefactors.
Teach me to count as true wealth
surplus of service given above services and goods consumed.

Save me from taking advantage of the long lease
of selfishness
which inherited wealth puts in the hands of every heir.

May I by thrift always have more than I immediately need,
keep it prudently invested,
and give generously to worthy persons and causes.
Grant me either poverty or riches,
or if it may be, a modest competence,
according as one or another of these conditions will best
fit me for your service.
Save me from the base desire to gain money by the chance or
certainty of others' loss.

Make me friendly to all such well-considered changes
in the holding, distribution, and transmission of property
as will relieve the material misery of extreme poverty,
prevent the spiritual dangers of extreme wealth,
and give to the greatest number a fair opportunity
to enjoy the material and spiritual advantages of toil
and comfort
without grinding want or debilitating luxury.

Fellowship

Father of All Mercies

I thank you for groups of congenial persons
with whom to talk,
and feast,
and laugh,
and sing,
and play,
and cast off care.

May I ever be ready to give my best to my friends,
and to receive from them the best they have to give in this
happy mutual exchange.

While the size and complexion of groups which can meet with
mutual profit is limited by manners,
cultivation,
and community of interest,
may I avoid the spirit of exclusiveness as the deadliest
poison of the soul.

May I make the circle of my friends as large as possible,
sincerely regretting the exclusion of any
whom lack of fitness or congeniality compels me to keep out,
never forgetting that the door of exclusiveness,
whether arrogantly slammed,
or gently closed under regretful necessity,
always shuts me out from infinitely more than it shuts
in with me.

While doing my best to contribute to the common joy,
may I heartily rejoice when others,
more rich,
more brilliant,
more resourceful,
make greater contributions.

Save me alike from jealous pride over my points
of fancied superiority,
and foolish sensitiveness about my points of inferiority.

Save me from the folly of trying to make society
the substantial food of life,
instead of its spice and sauce,
and from the hollowness of heart and bitterness
of spirit
which are the penalties of such perversity.

May I first of all earn my place in society by doing
some honest work,
and filling some useful place in industry,
scholarship,
politics,
art,
or philanthropy,
and then use my influence to have fellowship
in simplicity of life,
in reasonableness of hours,
in moderation of expense,
in the rational recreation
of the evenings and holidays
with those whose mornings and ordinary days
are devoted to doing their fair share of the world's hard work.

Country

God of Our Fathers

I thank you for my country—
its liberties and laws,
its institutions and traditions,
its courts and schools,
its executive officers and legislators,
its army and navy,
its civil servants and police.

May I honor every department of it,
and every one who serves it faithfully.
May I obey its laws.
May I pay my taxes cheerfully,
glad of the opportunity to contribute my full proportion
of the means whereby it is maintained.
May I form intelligent opinions of public policy,
and express them in earnest discussion and a disinterested vote.
May I commend faithful public servants wherever
commendation is deserved,
and condemn those who pervert political office or influence to
selfish ends.
May I work with the party which on the whole best
represents the policy which I approve,
not expecting perfection either in men or measures;
yet may I stand ready to leave my party
when its opponents offer substantially better men or better
measures.

Having first solved my individual problems
in the support of myself, and those dependent on me,
may I accept whatever public office,
service or trust my fellow-citizens may confer.
May I seek whatever office or position I feel qualified to fill
better than it would otherwise be filled,
counting no sacrifice of
time,
money,
leisure,
or personal convenience too great,
if thereby I may return to my community and country
a little part of the countless benefits they have bestowed
on me.
May my love of country include love of state and town,
and prompt me to do my fair share of local political work.

May it also involve a kindly interest in the welfare of every
other country,
and the effort to substitute arbitration for war,
and to maintain a just peace with all the other nations.

Judgment

Just and Righteous Judge of All

As often as I seek the hard good above me,
as often as I repent the easy evil into which I fall,
so often you are with me to approve and to forgive.

Thereby may I be lifted up above too great concern for what
men say of me.

Still human praise is dear,
and the blame of others is hard to bear.

May I strive to deserve my friends' approval,
and when I fail may I be more sorry for the fault than
for the blame it brings.

When through no fault of mine I am condemned;
when I turn from the outgrown truth and outworn right
of yesterday
to the unproved truth and untried right of tomorrow;
when I stand loyally by the hidden goodness in men who are
called bad;
when I sacrifice the nearby good which everybody sees
for the far-off good which most people cannot see;
when in a just economy I appear mean,
or for higher efficiency indulge in what looks like luxury;
when I obey your specific call within,
instead of the common clamor without;

when in strenuous intensity of service I seem over-ambitious,
or in prudent self-preservation seem indolent—
at all such times may I rest secure in your understanding
of my inmost purpose, and your charity for my shortcomings.

Help me to judge others on this same generous scale—
counting him highest who with most love fulfills the duties
of his station,
be that station high or low;
counting him lowest who succeeds in getting most
and giving least.

Give me sympathy for all the poor,
whether their poverty be that of purse, or talent, or culture,
or opportunity.

May I have eyes to see the worth that shines through coarse
circumstance,
rude manners,
ruined reputation,
and repented sin.

Yet may I ever hold in highest honor those who in great
wealth and high station serve you and their fellowmen with
a generous aim and a humble heart.

Bereavement

Lord of Life and Death

You bind us to life by sweet, tender ties—
father,
mother,
brother,
sister,
husband,
wife,
son,
daughter,
friend.
All the tendrils of my heart are twined around them;
all my purposes revolve about them;
all my hopes are centered in them;
all my success is measured by their joy.

You take them away.

Then I am tempted to withdraw altogether from the world,
in hopeless dejection,
a burden to myself and a sorrow to my remaining friends;
or hide myself in foreign lands,
or plunge madly into meaningless activities,
vainly striving to run away from the grief I never can escape.

Make me strong to resist this cowardice.
Forbid that I should idly accept my dear one's mortality.

In the hour of sore bereavement may I summon the great
resources of the soul—
memory,
imagination,
faith,
hope,
love.

May I gratefully recall all that my beloved one was to me,
all that he stood for in the world.

May I live even more constantly in the companionship
of his spirit;
may I carry out in the old spheres in which we together moved,
as much of his purpose as I can.
May I be kind to the friends he loved,
devoted to the community in which he lived,
loyal to the causes which he served.

Thus in my life may he still live on,
to my own comfort,
and the welfare of the world.

By loyally living in the perpetual presence of my dear departed
may I gain the power to see you who are invisible,
and to realize your presence,
that those whom you have taken may not only remain
with me,
but also draw me nearer to you.

Immortality

Immortal, Everlasting Father

Though fidelity of soul can do much to rob the grave
of its victory,
still I too must soon follow the dear ones gone before.
For them and for myself
I crave more than a transient survival in loyal hearts
who take up and carry on our work.

For this true immortality I turn in entire confidence to you.
I know not how, out of a world which gave no evidence
of anything but matter and force,
you have called forth the life and love which are
its crowning ornaments.
I know no more, and no less, of how you can lead these
broken lives
and severed loves of ours to the fulfillment they demand.
But all I know of love in myself,
all I see of it in human hearts,
makes me confident that you will this fulfillment.

As without other souls to love I should shrink
into nothingness,
so, apart from souls to love and be loved by in return,
you would not be Father,
and would be less than I know you to be.

Because I cannot think of you as less than myself,
or lower than the highest men and women I have known,
therefore I trust your heart of love
to preserve all that is precious in these lives and loves
of ours.

I thank you for reported visions of departed ones;
yet I would not place on these material props
more weight than they will bear.

My confidence is in you as you are revealed in my own soul,
in humanity at its best,
and in Jesus Christ.

As you have made this life of ours on earth a closed circle,
free from violent interruptions,
may I accept it as the call to concentrate my little strength
on life and love and duty as I find them here during
my brief sojourn,
trusting my loved ones and myself entirely to your power,
your wisdom,
and your love,
for future growth in character and progress in blessedness.

Charity

Father of Grace and Goodness

In all my yearning after immortality,
teach me to prize quality above quantity,
and to measure the value of duration
by the kind of life with which each day is filled.

You are love to all:
rich,
poor,
high,
low,
good,
bad;
and charity—
the power to live in and for lives other than one's own—
is the open door through which my life enters into
and abides in yours.

Towards those who are stronger, happier, better,
may I look up in ardent admiration
and enthusiastic devotion,
never letting envy or jealousy rob me of the share in their
excellence which belongs to every one who heartily
rejoices in it.

Towards those more poor,
more wretched,

more wicked than myself,
may I go out in generous aid,
tactful compassion,
kindly counsel,
according to their needs—
never letting pride or self-righteousness hold me back
from doing for the worst man
the kindest thing his character and my ability permit.

Save me from the obvious hypocrisy of offering charity
without the physical act,
the material article,
which is its practical expression.

Save me from the more subtle hypocrisy
of giving money or goods without the sympathetic sharing of
life's problems which gifts of goods and money,
if they are to bless rather than curse,
must judiciously express.
Sharing the joys and honors of the more favored,
bearing the burdens and sorrows of the less fortunate,
may I so multiply my life by all the other lives I touch,
that it shall be large as its environment,
and constantly expanding with it;
may I have that quality of charity that Christ brought
to earth,
and, wherever lived,
makes the blessedness of heaven.